Tricks
High Up

with Afterword by Taiji Master Jef Crab

Margaret A. Harrell

ISBN (hard cover): 979-8-9871061-7-4
ISBN (pbk): 979-8-9904800-0-1

A Published in Heaven Series Book

Published in Heaven Books include titles by His Holiness The Dalai Lama, President Jimmy Carter, Thomas Merton, Seamus Heaney, Hunter S. Thompson, Jack Kerouac, Andy Warhol, Allen Ginsberg, Yoko Ono, William S. Burroughs, Edvard Munch, Diane di Prima, Jim Carroll, Amiri Baraka, Gregory Corso, John Updike, Rita Dove, Wendell Berry, David Amram, Douglas Brinkley, BONO, Ron Whitehead, Lawrence Ferlinghetti, and many more.

Published in conjunction with Saeculum University Press
of Sibiu Romania and Raleigh NC

For inquiries, signed copies, and speaking requests,
contact marharrell@hotmail.com

https://margaretharrell.com

Praise for Margaret A. Harrell's books

Selected Review Snippets

JUST OUT: *Beyond 3-D*
Keep This Quiet! III—rev. ed.

"Margaret Ann Harrell's book of initiations is a golden bough, a sacred marriage, an initiation, a wake, a book of revelation, a literary and spiritual journey into and through an ever expanding universal consciousness. Margaret Ann Harrell's BEYOND 3-D is her Big Book, her epic narrative poetic masterpiece.

"Brilliant as a literary and psychoanalytic and spiritual text, it is a deeply touching and vulnerable human story. A book that breaks new ground by combining and weaving together such a broad spectrum of genres. I congratulate her on having the courage to write the book and share the book with the world."
>   —Ron Whitehead, Lifetime US Beat Poet Laureate

Keep This Quiet!

"Margaret Harrell's *Keep This Quiet!* offers an illuminating look at Hunter S. Thompson in full throttle trying to make it as a Top Notch prose-stylist. Harrell fills in many important biographical gaps. A welcome addition to what is becoming the HST cottage industry. Read it."
>   —Douglas Brinkley, editor of *The Proud Highway* and *Fear and*
>   *Loathing in America*

"With a solid dose of humor and another perspective on these writers from a personal friend, *Keep This Quiet!* is a moving read and much recommended to any literary studies or memoir collection."
>   —*Midwest Book Review*

"In the ever-expanding list of biographies and memoirs about Hunter S. Thompson, this latest offering, *Keep This Quiet!* by Margaret A. Harrell, is quite simply a breath of fresh air."
>   —Rory Patrick Feehan, PhD, owner of https://totallygonzo.org

"This is no ordinary book about or including Thompson. It's a memoir detailing personal relationships with three authors, the main focus being on Hunter . . . [I] must stress that this book, as a memoir is quite deep and holds the door open for the reader. While Hunter is a huge selling point, the book has the legs to stand alone."
— Martin Flynn, owner of https://hstbooks.org

Keep <u>This</u> Quiet Too!

"A passionately written memoir that doesn't sit around being fit and proper and strait-laced . . . As a key to the lives of these three writers it is idiosyncratic and in an age where blandness is the norm it is a pleasure to go on her journey and find out a little about what makes these men tick and what drove her to them."
— Eric Jacobs, *Beat Scene* (print) magazine, UK

Keep This Quiet! III—*first ed.*: Initiations

"This is the third and highly recommended title in Margaret Harrell's outstanding *Keep This Quiet!* autobiographical series. A fascinating and exceptionally well written personal story, *Keep This Quiet! III: Initiations* is as informative as it is entertaining and will be especially interesting to students of Jungian psychology and metaphysics. *Keep This Quiet! III: Initiations* is very highly recommended for both community and academic library collections. Also exceptionally commended are the first two volumes in this outstanding series."
— *Midwest Book Review*

Keep This Quiet! IV—rev. ed.: Ancient Secrets Revealed

"Margaret Harrell is a skilled professional writer with excellent ability to communicate and weave esoteric ideas about science, psychology, philosophy, and spirituality. Richard Unger's channeled hand analysis description of her as a 'grand synthesizer' was apt and accurate."
— Ron Rattner, subject of *Walks with Rob: A Spiritual Memoir* documentary

Space Encounters III revised—
Inserting Consciousness into Collisions

"A wizard of turning the sign language of the specifics into messages of the beyond . . . A fantastic journey into the source of creativity. Another re-story-ing of how our lives are entangled in the grandiose web of the universe. This time taken from a myriad of perspectives: quantum leaps and how they shake up the Newtonian mechanistic worldview, Jungian archetypal wisdom seen from a quite unique angle, the huge impact on a life's course starting with childhood imprints, spicy poetic wordplay endowed with meaning...a writer who composes symphonies of words and dances along the cosmic plot lines she is detecting. This is heralding a new style of life where the old story is no longer valid, the narrative of warmongers and suppression coming to an end. A new story is revealed paradoxically containing and rebirthing ancient wisdom. A re-story-ing of how the grand web of the universe is entangled with our personal lives boiling down to that marvelous gem that tells us all living beings matter to the grand web. The whole journey is a wake-up call: what you do, matters and impacts the cosmos . . . Creation is a creative act and we are all involved. Read this book as an eye-opener, I-opener, beyond the eye/I. Join the dance of *Space Encounters* III!"

—Chris Van de Velde, Belgium coach of coaches

"Finally, a manual of the Universe but also connected to the deep psychology of the human being . . . . The magic of this book is that it positions our place in the universe and our dream of life with much more clarity. A manual indeed."

—Jef Crab, Tai Chi master and Taoist

To the Twenty-first Century

"Flyers" for those who advanced

iv
v
i
i i i i
i

i

—pāst "Go"—"

i

"otherwise

"

past "Go"

Ahead of TIME
If there we find you, these

"Flyers"

may be—

if not the ticket,

then clarification.

Or otherwise essential

CARRY-

ONS[1]

Trying to assemble

---

[1] *ons*—ours (NL)

and not dis-semble

the right arm of

the 21st Century DE-

FENCE

system

Why is it a

de-FENCE

System

Fencing the stolen for the genuine . . .

It belongs to the 21st century

de-

FENCE

system

to Humanity its owners, its allegiance,

how

dare it be put

on the mark-et AS A

FENCED

*b7♮——½

T aim

item[2]

Having found some

CARRY-

ONS

of value

to try the

:n to place them in range of readers

CARRY-

ONS

or "ours"
IERE

WHERE

in All Time, perhaps aeons away,

"carr̶y̶-̶A̶N̶G̶E̶R̶S̶Y̶-̶
not-inevitable,̶
worked with to re-sh-

All Time, perhaps aeons away,
 to try then to place them in range of

 gettable

worked with to re-sh-

ape the

not-inevitable

"carry-

ons

now noted as

being

delivered

Thank you, spirits, and/or unknown technology from the future, for arriving here in my apartment, landing without a ship, or not even landing, working from an airy nothingness to operate my computer.

Jane Roberts, *Seth Speaks*
Chapter 19: Session 575, March 24, 1971

Since past, present, and future do not exist, this is a level of crystal-clear communication of consciousness. Those involved have an excellent knowledge of their own backgrounds and histories, of course, but in this state possess also a much larger perspective, in which private and historical backgrounds are seen as a portion of a greater perceivable whole.

(9:35.) At this level, messages literally flash through the centuries from one great man or woman to another. The future speaks to the past. The great artists have always been able to communicate at this level and while living literally operated at this level of consciousness a good deal of the time. Only the most exterior portions of their personalities bowed to the dictates of historical period.

For those who reach this state and utilize it, communication is clearest. It must be understood that this communication works in both ways. Leonardo da Vinci knew of Picasso, for example. There are great men and women who go unknown. Their contemporaries ignore them. Their achievements may be misunderstood or physically lost, but at this level of consciousness they share in these communications, and at another level of existence their achievements are recognized.

I do not mean to imply, however, that only the great share in this communication of consciousness. (Pause.) A great simplicity is necessary, and out of this, many of the most lowly in men's terms also share in these communications. There is an unending conversation going on throughout the universe, and a most meaningful one. (Long pause.) Those from both your past and your future have a hand in your present world, and at this level the problems that have been met and will be encountered are being discussed. This is the heart of communication. It is most usually encountered either in a protected deep level of sleep or in a sudden spontaneous trance state. Great energy is generated.

Theseus

More strange than true; I never may believe
These antique fables, nor these fairy toys.
Lovers and madmen have such seething brains,
Such shaping fantasies, that apprehend
More than cool reason ever comprehends.
The lunatic, the lover, and the poet
Are, of imagination, all compact.
One sees more devils than vast hell can hold—
That is, the madman. The lover all as frantic,
Sees Helen's beauty in a brow of Egypt.
The poet's eye, in fine frenzy rolling,
Doth glance from heaven to earth, from earth to heaven.
And as imagination bodies forth
The forms of things unknown, the poet's pen
Turns them to shapes, and gives to airy nothing
A local habitation and a name.

So we will also be looking for, in the spiral arm of the Milky
Way galaxy we are in, the arm of our Information this century. We
will put our noses to the ground to sense it—our Information
CONTINGENT.

My proposal means accepting that information is a genuine physical quantity that can be traded by "informational forces" in the same way that matter can be moved around by physical forces. It also means accepting complexity as a physical variable. With real causal efficacy, rather than a merely qualitative description of how complicated a system is. I believe it is only under the action of an informational law that the information channel, or software control, associated with the genetic code could have come into existence.

I may have made my proposal seem more radical than it is. The idea of informational, or software, laws isn't all that new. Many other investigators have suggested something similar. For example, [Nobel Prize winner] Manfred Eigen has written, "Our task is to find an algorithm, a natural law, that leads to the origin of information."

—Paul Davies, *The Fifth Miracle*

Contents

Author's Note

OK. That was "mind through matter" at the computer. Pure and simple. Spirit "sat"—rather, the "mind," the "tricks high up," of spirit sat—at the computer. Did it by stepping mentally into the juncture between computer and printer. Intercepted the instruction at that juncture, to be exact. If the instruction was, "Jump," it might order: "Stay still." If the instruction was: "Print a whole page"—which was actually the instruction—this "mind through matter" in control might lift out a few sentences to print, rearranged or lightly added to with "signatures," as I called them—initials, for example—beside a word. The rest of the page text saved for later. Or never at all. Or for the time when normalcy returned, which was not likely. Not in this apartment, with its overseers. Not then, the 1990s.

But why go so far back? In a timeless realm, there is no "back," only the "mind," the "spirit," positioning—aligning information with events on the way. Yes, that's right, not events already here—events going down the tube. Slowly, at that.

Crisscrossing through time, it arrived, unknown, where no one had thought to try to direct the computer mentally.

Knocking again at my doorstep in 2022, spirit "committees" showed up again in my home, now in Raleigh, North Carolina, in urgent insistence that they were my path to healing. The

Universe is not above using health issues to crack its whip. It gave me one. Immediately, thought, a healing dangled over my head, a health spur. Seated on it, the crux of the healing, was this returning 1990s material, like dolls suddenly dancing at night on a shelf when the room was empty.

I dived delightedly into that "lost" material, relishing the privilege of looking back at a once-me, listening attentively—intrigued—because as I modify, understand, update her messages here now, she challenges my consciousness—to say the least.

Emerging from no-time—left unfinished during the extravaganza, alone in my Tienen apartment the entire ten years of the 1990s, reinforced now by a new spirit committee updating—the channeled material is clearly *aimed for now*, at *pinpointed* spots in the Earth. It always was, I see in hindsight, as this me gears up to meet the task at hand.

And thus some carry-ons came to sit with me, setting the course for this book.

Back to 1999. In just a few years the concept of "ending" would be headed far out to sea, increasingly distant from the energies of concern now. Going backward and backward, into time, perhaps adding distance to the square of this or the diameter of that. But just for now—*just for now* (as Ending has a particular meaning and Beginning too)—*it is highly energized to speak from a fairly extensive, vocal voice*. What ended, and what did it have to say, in a last-ditch effort to make itself count, to bring to light more of the Light it had held, some of it obscure to us? Too bright or too dim for us to concern ourselves with. To our peril.

These carry-ons, then, coming to be chosen from as the Departure picked up. And the Earth left the course it was on. *And there, at the intersection, much was missed, unremarked on.*

I stopped. I asked myself, *was there anything to see*? Here, at the precisely predicted Ending. And from there, a Beginning. And did I have something shored in, carried maybe for centuries—or that I somehow, glancing in just the right spot, found in me, from centuries before? Did I have a "comment"—a closing Note? Was there something important to me about it?

Or did I have no pertinence to it? Should I better hurry on into the new? Who knew if a thousand years from now it would have been the more important choice? Still, to get there—standing at the Alpha-Omega Gate, Gate-AU—as Baudelaire ambles in to say he dropped this clue to us in a word (*gateaux*)—I look to see if something had remained the same for this purpose, and this moment, that might draw some use of this space *in me*.

Watching the dimensions fly past Physical. Abstract. Alpha. Omega. Alpha-Omega. A unit of time. A UNIT OF SPACE. A unit of Lifetime. Lifetime in the spacetime of the entire history of the planet, circling through spacetime in the time/eternity of the planet

What can we say that no one else can say?

Remember, we are approaching the question of whether there is something like a "DNA" or sequence-control, for things like electricity.

Part One

Then and Now:

As the Twentieth Century

Drew to a Close

1997

Tienen, Belgium

Backtracking to Catch Some

Readers Up

For some time now, I strove to get my extraordinary experiences (happening daily) accredited by a *scientific* readership. But no. Technology, the experts said—only *we*, with software, can control it. *Thought* cannot. And definitely it cannot spring upon a person sitting at the printer. (Ha, ha, *laughed AI from the future. But that was invisible then. To most.*)

You don't say. Ha-ha again. I shouted till I was red in the face in the 1990s. To no avail. *Look, we humans can do this,* I screamed. No and no again. *Let us keep working in technology. Let us give machines our fragile place in the Earth, up to a point. Let us shut our eyes to our own future options. Let's go blindly, like sheep, into a mechanical world.* Ha-ha and ha-ha, scientists cajoled back. *Of course, you cannot work the computer with spirit-driven energy. What kind of force is that?*

Let's see. Is it one of the weak forces we didn't yet discover? A particle, like the God particle, but with undetected abilities that operate in our world? An escapee from 4-D? From 15-D? That's it. Maybe some unknown abilities we might use from

3

there descended from subtle-energy helicopters to alert whoever would listen, and I did. I was spellbound. Hypnotized.

Wait. Wait. Are you going to believe it's inevitable and normal for technology to outpace humans? Not even give humans a chance? Think of the long path of evolution we've taken.

Now, in 2023, the course they announce/chart for us humans reverses. Just wait, they say:

> *Imagine being able to make a machine do your bidding with your thoughts alone, no button pressing, typing, screen tapping or fumbling with remote controls, just brain power. Well, this sci-fi scenario could be closer to reality than you think.*[1]

So back to me, and these *precursor* bulletins I tried hard to bring attention to—experiences as real as the sun rising in the sky each morning. They might, says the BBC, *in just a few years* become commonplace as what is "real" and what concocted with software and AI become almost indistinguishable.

I do trust that "almost" will always create a distance between us and "it." However, by what miniscule measuring tool will most of us be able to make the detection?

Meanwhile, denounced or unknown, a fiesta of precursor experiences, *as just demonstrated*, ran through the energy day after day, minute after minute, in my apartment 24/7 in Belgium in the 1990s, trying—I now realize—to get ahead of AI. No kidding. A transplant into my apartment giving advance notice. And not waiting till the future gave permission. Let

4

Uncertainty come in and at least admit that inside its borders such nontechnology spirit "technology" exists, I pursued. But no. A flat no. *You are telling us something we have no proof of.*

So it was just the computer and me—no programs involved—*no animal experimentation*—no electrodes in my brain—with whatever spirit energy was participating, creating these rearranged texts, assuring me in demonstrations that mind through matter was real.

I appealed my case. Might I speak at an international para-psychological conference? Yes, I sent out a request. No dice.

At my wit's end, *now that I had proved sufficiently* TO MYSELF *exactly what the position is and that I didn't make it up,* I contemplated taking the whimsical *approach that I made the extraordinary experiences* that now outnumber the unextraordinary up, *that they are pure fabrications of mine (misguided perspectives governed by and substantiated by proof before my very eyes); let's see if the style that allows me is more interesting,*

I will not have to postpone the trip I am embarked on, *waiting for the rest of the travelers to join in. I will go on, pretending everything extremely unusual I experience is imaginary.* So only those who can follow to this point—or want to try to: one, two, three, or ten, or dozens or thousands; I am not counting—will right away come along. But the good news is, I can plunge ahead into the cave of treasures, open the unknown caskets of jewels—see what trails into the future lead off from here. A different future than if I do not proceed this way, looking behind these closed doors. And had I dillydallied longer, AI would have beat me to it! We are in a race, AI and I. And there are—of course— some I can meet up ahead (to whom this psychic business is all ho-hum), starting like this. And doubtless some few even right at my side, contemporary. But if I do not, I will be trapped interminably here, waiting for a

consensus to declare that my experiences are officially real; that is, that "I" am. But there is another consensus I can reach by not waiting: I will not be Godot. Anyway, Nabokov studied butterflies, and considering that the "butterfly effect" (coined in 1972 shortly before his death—not by him) was then en route, even there perhaps the Universe is making a point. Who am I to try to look that far ahead?

So began the next step.

I put the paper into the printer tray, flick the printer on and off. Something unprogrammed comes out: the printer

[Threshing-floors: 2 Chronicles 3:1]:
Then Solomon began to build the house
of the Lord at Jerusalem in mount
Moriah, where the Lord appeared to
David his father, in the place that David
had prepared in the threshingfloor of
Ornan the Jeubsite.

on this. The

new idea pouring through me "Nabokov would

have said he made the whole thing up," the line originally read, on-screen; isolated, it is moved prominently to the top of the printed page.

Just like Debussy *trying to write music in images*, using "arpeggio, pedal-point, staccato," etc., to mimic the movement of water;[2] or Pointillist painters using dots; or musicians in the late nineteenth/early twentieth centuries branching out into the octonic; or Rimsky Korsakov, using a scale of music the ears were not accustomed to—the twelve-tone scale—I sense the artist mode as nearby. My workshop of apprentices, like that of Peter Paul Rubens but minimalized, nano format, will be at the computer, *hidden behind our inability to see beyond a narrow range of Light*. Or perhaps Rembrandt is a good example—the small degrees of visible light he put into paintings, incorporating many shades of black in *sprezzatura*, Seeming carelessness. Well, what if, in a come-back, invisible at that, he took all the visible light out—working in invisible light, not reflected by the eye.

Then as if Rembrandt turned on a light switch, a painting popped out that we could see, crafted from invisible frequencies. But we didn't see that either. Nor did we see Rembrandt, who began to wish he had never taken on this task of working—too soon by our count—in the Invisible Realm. But hold on, this is only 2023. Wait a bit longer. As I don't know the rules here, I am allowed to say whatever I wish.

And perhaps, or surely, it is I who am the apprentice.

And don't forget. I am making it up. Even as you see strange-looking printed-out pages, cast your eyes into the *to-be-refuted* category. Do not believe a single sight.

<u>July 2022</u>

Hold it. One last fact check. Mid-January 1991, I bought my first computer. Late 2001, I packed up and left Belgium to return to the United States? I repeat, "every day" in between, the printer, forced to step out of a mechanical mode, produced not the on-screen text I was staring at on the computer screen display, but a lavish variation, ornate, baroque: a "Bach" counterpoint behind the scenes. Setting up a focus, it lifted just a phrase high up on the page to draw it into a spotlight. Programmed, of course? No.

Not possible without programming!

The objections pour in from the entire mighty science community. What is the cause that creates the effect. Tell us that, will you? There must be a repeatable physical agent as "cause"—no? No.

> You are a child with the power of telekinesis. Using only your mind, you must manipulate various objects to escape the laboratory where you are held captive. This is the premise for *Awakening*, a virtual reality experience developed by American neurotech startup Neurable. In order to play, a headband must be worn with **six electrodes** that register the brain's activity—they allow the user to control the first-person video game via thoughts, emulating the protagonists' superpowers. Brain wave sensors of the sort used to play *Awakening* were developed for research and medical applications,

but they have already demonstrated their potential in video game control.

In general, neurotechnology aims to connect the mind with machines via brain-computer interfaces (BCIs) . . .

After a calibration phase in which the program familiarizes itself with the users' brain, the BCI can link specific brain waves—identified by their frequency and location—with predetermined actions . . . if the user concentrates on moving forward, the program executes an advance, if the user concentrates on turning right, the program executes a right turn. In this way, mind-control has been used to steer wheelchairs, toy vehicles and even telepresence robots before finally making it to video games.

That's in "Video Games Controlled by Thought," March 4, 2020.[3]

It's in January 1991 that my experience started—anchored in the premise *what I was doing was not a hallucination, it was possible*. Not a fluke, but just one of the Revelations in Waiting for us humans around a mind-bending corner or two. Of course, only bent minds need apply.

The above examples were the earliest expressions of what I fondly call "computer PK": short for "psychokinesis" (or "telekinesis"): "the movement of physical objects by the mind"—yes—like spoon bending.

As soon as I set my first computer up in the Tienen, Belgium, living room, it began. I was, the first time, warned:

by a nonphysical bell newly "residing" in my apartment since the death of my boyfriend, Willy van Luyten. It rang like a consolation prize, making me think of the Patrick Swayze character in the then-newly-released movie *Ghosts*, who hung around ingeniously after his murder.

I was not the only one to hear it. Even four PhD friends of mine, visiting in my apartment from the United States, heard it. Repeatedly. And wrote brief witness statements.

Trained in logic, they knew what was what.

Preceding the first arrival, it rang, telling me something was up—to pay attention, hark, heed this: *not to think the computer was broken but* LEAVE IT TURNED ON. *Look carefully at what would imminently occur.* So I did. In that first instance, after that a slew of blank pages spewed out, then an altered-text page, with a short phrase at the top—the word count vastly curtailed, as if there were judges deciding which words got to stay.

My mind drifted back to Zurich! For an explanation of the off-Earth annotation of my text—that is, the "signed" numbers (cf., "86X") inserted beside a word—did the Thompson's Chain-Reference Bible I bought in 1985 relate? It had sat on a shelf ever since. *If you know this story, don't worry. I will be extra brief.*

Did the inserted *numbers* correlate to the annotation numbers in the concordance? But how could light set out *toward* a future need? Gear itself up to exist *then*, when it had no apparent purpose at the time? You think that's not possible?

Well, after experimenting with a single atom going down a grating path, a professor of physics at Australian National University says otherwise (*Nature Physics*):

The researchers randomly added a second laser grating. They found that when this was present, the atoms created the wavelike interference pattern. When the second grating was not there, the atoms behaved like particles and traveled along a single path.

However, whether or not the second grating was added was determined *only after the atom had made it through the first crossroads.* The wave-like or particle-like behavior of the atom only came into existence when the researchers measured it *after it had completed its journey.*

This, says Andrew Truscott, shows that *"a future event causes the photon to decide its past."*[4] (my italics)

What? Whoa! How about that? In our world, we carefully divide up past-present-future, but the particle world, which makes up a dimension of it, doesn't listen. Did you hear me? It closes its ears to this rule.

Back then, beginning in 1984, I had happily enrolled at the C. G. Jung Institute in Zurich. At that point, as "the gods" would have it, an initiation whammed into my life. A cosmic spirit guide was the instigator. Consequently.

Which brings us to an afternoon in downtown Zurich, in 1985.

Again, if you know this story, don't worry. I will be brief.

As I arrived at Paradeplatz (Parade Square), my mind asso-ciated "Parade Square" with *a Blakenberge, Belgium, parade* , four years earlier. We are deep into the past now, but the "future" was "setting up." Par-ah-dah/Parade. Yes. Go on.

Not a smell or a picture—my verbal hemisphere of the brain was getting the hang of how association stimulated memory—a word brought it back, the veiled, energized picture inside. The Blankenberge incident, though numinous, had not revealed to me why, in 1985, it was numinous. But I couldn't dispute the fact that it was. Later information, however, showed that the parade was bringing—more or less synchronized—the Other World's announcement to me of the totally unexpected, by me, consciously at least, death of Milton Klonsky, who, living in a top-floor New York City walk-up, Apartment 9, around the corner from me in the mid-1960s, had squired me around the Village, being my quasi-romantic mentor.

Jung and others had been known to "visit" people in spirit just around the moment of death. So the Universe crafted a symbol to speed over to me, a parade, that I later found out was carrying this news. In particular, of how I should take his reception after death.

I will be brief. Holding up banners that read, CHILDREN OF NEPTUNE, SONS AND DAUGHTERS OF NEPTUNE, the marchers celebrated in a victorious atmosphere. Rejoicing. That was clear to me. And the numinosity. Upon their reaching me, what was my surprise? They paraded past to the end of the block but, veering neither right nor left, *turned back and marched again right in front of me.* As the North Sea winds pounded the ocean that wintry day in 1981, alone with my mini dachshund, that simple act of pointedly reappearing in front of me, in the numinosity, struck me as astounding.

16

Captured, branded, sure it was significant, I had no intimation consciously that he was at St. Vincent's Hospital over 2,600 miles away. No clue percolated over into my consciousness from New York City, even that he was sick. So I racked up this event as inexplicably numinous. Soon afterwards this wonderstruck moment caused me to retitle my then-twenty-years-in-progress "big book" *Love in Transition: The Voyage of Ulysses: Letters to Penelope.*

Later, I had a dream in which Milton told me he was "coming back." How baffling!

In those early stages of my consciousness expansion, how could I believe such a prediction? But I did (at least in half of me. Never mind the skeptical half).

Jump from November 1981 (his death date) to September 1985: my studio apartment in Zurich. Daily, I commuted on the short train ride along Lake Zurich to the Jung Institute in Küsnacht.

Here, in Zurich, he set up "classes" for me, in consciousness, making his first "appearance" in 1985, though by then in a much larger entity form, backed by, I suppose, or melted into, a group.

Now, a little background. Milton had been? A writer of literary nonfiction who had nine—YES, nine—fellowships at the MacDowell Colony for artists in New Hampshire. But more to the point, besides being in an almost-unheard-of high spiritual stratosphere, he so integrated it he could weave lofty intellect into spiritual witticisms of untold depth and had "an IQ that could stutter your butter," as author Seymour Krim put it. Krim located "the whole of Western civilization between his eyebrows . . . In fact, most of the noble repertoire

17

of English-speaking verse sprang to his dark purplish cracked lips at appropriate moments," when he wasn't "electrically bit[ing] out the language of the ballpark and streets."[5]

Back to the computer-PK.

By 1991, I had exited expensive Zurich for reasonably priced Belgium, the dollar having taken a dip. Having married a Belgian in 1970—and separated from him in 1983—I was automatically granted the privilege of dual national, US/Belgian citizenship. But there was a secondary reason I moved to Tienen.

Love. I'd fallen for Willy Van Luyten in 1987. Now in the wee hours of a foggy January 7, 1991 (Old Christmas, the Feast of the Epiphany), he suddenly died. I continued living in his apartment, and it stirred with happenings; not "a creature" was silent; notably, the nonphysical bell seemed to tap into thoughts and communicate with me or with select friends by ringing to say, *Yes, I agree,* Or *Danger! Something is happening in the back room!* Or that a page was going to print—wait for it—with irregular text display. But the "bell ringers" brought an opportunity for much wider communication.

The computer-PK demonstrations immediately commenced work with me. They hammered into my brain that *no sentence, no thought, sits itself down in the context that was there before it "was born."* In fact, it births a new context with it, a variation of what "used to be," seconds earlier. *Every single instance of anything sets itself in a brand-new focal point. A single context lasts only as long as the instant it is perceived.* Like time, it keeps moving. It does this by assimilating into "where" it was before "existing"—now shifting the focus. And focus shift after focus shift *defined* the printouts.

18

I advised myself: *Take a look.* Do *the numbers inserted beside* THAT *word align* with the *Thompson Bible references*? Take a look. Well, *yes*.

Many would have found them annoying. Not me!

I thrived on how the repetitive linear clock stopped, replaced by a speed that, though faster than we could follow, balanced itself with awareness. And awareness, as fast as it became aware, yet slowed in our sense of time by boring into a focus. I loved *not knowing* what would slide out of the computer.

The initial text they pounced on was for *Commentary* magazine managing editor Marion Magid, an assignment to write "The Milton Klonsky I Knew."

December 25, 2022
Jef

In a conversation Christmas Day 2022, via Skype with Jef Crab, my 1990s Taiji master in Belgium, who is now living on the edge of the rainforest in Suriname, a shaman and Taoist, a wise man, we got onto a topic very relevant here. To listen to Jef speak, I get into a quiet, meditative frame of mind, always. It happens automatically. He speaks in kindness, surrounded by a deep silence, backed by nature, trees, wood, bees, a coffee plantation:

"*All creativity will reshape us.*"

He went on:

> because it will reorganize our energetic complex. And the energetic complex is the vehicle which *will automatically absorb these creative energies.*

Creativity is *not from us.*

With each sentence carrying weight, he next said, also to ponder:

> *The creative forces exist on another level, a much more subtle level.*

He was speaking to my recent healing from a life-threatening illness in 2022. I knew, I had just said, the creative energy was healing me. "And the other energy would kill me."

I meant, a focus on being sick would.

Not only would it have brought my mood down, but it would also have *prevented* my healing. I knew that intuitively, immediately, upon getting the diagnosis. Somewhere inside me, I had this information. In fact, all my energy since my diagnosis seemed blazingly intent on bringing out new books, as if that was the purpose of getting ill. It instantly swept in and began reorganizing my inner living space, taking up occupancy in my brain, my awareness, my spirit.

It brought me a message to start on these 1990s manuscripts, *as if "someone" had calculated I would need the time I "had left" to get through the important ones.* AND, it seemed to say, they had—why else bother?—an audience waiting. Who knew? Well, *they* knew when giving me this material in the first place. I hadn't been thinking like that. I had all the time in the world, didn't I? Ah, delusion we live in.

A Grand Calculator began ruling out some of my current choices as irrelevant in the grand scheme of things.

Jef pinpointed it as "creativity." Of course, behind that was this spirit energy.

"And it's up to humanity, and each of us, to ask," he said:

> Will I *really try to realize my dignity*? Or will I *get stuck in the field and all the diminishing forces*? . . .

"In fact," he went on, "being infected with the Ebola virus was one of the best experiences of my life. I was in this big bright creative energy." He added that using the creative energy can be in the garden, teaching Taiji . . . Whatever takes us into those energies that are beyond our everyday level, where we find—"

"—connections," I finished.

I found out about the lump in my breast—long gone now but alarmingly conspicuous then—by feeling it, and first of course questioning my find. *Was it the way I was standing? Was it a muscle from ballet?* Of course it was not. It didn't go away. So my outer life got directed to addressing it with the medical community. I, on the other hand, didn't focus on it, kept any worries at bay, but told myself: *Two months. You have two months before they begin treatment. Use them wisely. Bring out those shelved manuscripts given to you in Tienen and also in the light body seminars inside the spirit guide energy. It's time for a command performance.*

※

I went to sleep perplexed, having typed the 1997 text that opens this book.

I didn't like the next text. But when I woke, a penciled arrow in the original 1999 manuscript indicated to delete a large section. Had it been there the night before? Presumably. But why hadn't I seen it? Why had my mind skipped right over it if it was there, and the odds are it was (I agree)?

Anyway, this morning the little pencil arrow was conspicuous, and I followed the cut—to here.

1997, Tienen, Belgium

In one of my favorite stories, The Metamorphosis, Kafka's protagonist, Gregor Samsa, identified with a bug. Just as I now identify with these freakish experiences. I do not care whether they are real or not to another. They are my ticket to go further.

After all, Kafka did not miss the *entire experience of being Kafka*, for he identified with the uncertainty of being himself *before* what he was had been defined and labeled. No, *preceding that, he tried to label himself—before our "Kafka" existed*—identifying with how he looked, on the outside, were he to identify with *the inside* at this unheard-of state of preexistence.

Do not ask if I know what I am talking about. Not at all. I was just following the wormhole.

※

A funny thing is that I know I am famous. As in order for you to be famous, people have to know of you—for they make you famous—this sounds bizarre. But it isn't. Either I am famous in another universe, or I am famous in the future—or am around someone, in this energy field, who is very famous and putting that feeling into me. But no, I am famous. I am sure. I have the feeling of having signed autographs.

And perhaps I am in an antimatter field relative to the Earth, *contrarily placed to everything that is placed in any position here.* Or, an alternative, which can coexist with these, someone is imagining that I am famous, in order to make that come true—reinforcing probability by believing in the one probability that this is true, but letting me experience that future now, and in that way letting me conduct myself according to my most positive inner truth. It becomes so real to me, then, this conviction that I am

*p866Xfamous, relative to the people around me who

[Appeal taken; Acts 25:11]:

(Paul): For if I be an offender or have committed any thing worthy of death, I refuse not to die; but if there be none of these things whereof these accuse me, no man may deliver me unto them. I appeal unto Ceasar.

are famous, when I am invisibly famous. But famous somewhere, sometime, FOR SURE.

It occurs to me—I can feel it—St. Paul did not know he was famous, in the first century AD. Not from concrete proof. He had none. But remember the earlier quote about a particle "knowing its future."

> "This says Andrew Truscott, shows that *'a future event causes the photon to decide its past.'"*[6] (my italics)

But who can answer (when asked why you did what you did), "From inside, a particle convinced me to." No, many of us (not me) are sure we are on our own—even as perhaps the origin of information itself comes to get us. Or something spills out of the spiral Milky Way, and we happen to be looking "up." Or "things" were looking up that day, and so, optimistically we looked up. "Things" did it, though. They went first, in "looking up."

2023

I cut the rest of the previous thought. But famous in another universe? I don't want to delete the thought. My hands will not let me do it. For in a multiverse-universe concept, who knows but that it might exist? It is idle to try to pinpoint location in this matter—in this type of information-receipt. No, leave it there, hanging by a (quantum) string. Let's go on. Ha-ha. I will not tell you what I think about the matter.

<u>2022</u>

This long delay has caught up with me, grabbing me by the scuff of my neck: "Do you want to leave these heaps of channeled material thrown in a dump pile?" it demands. "Or see what mysteries they unfold for you?"

Before I left Belgium for the States, the printer sometimes produced outbursts of nonstop computer-PK, in a barrage, keyed to no page numbers or books—

And now it leads me back to them.

The Universe is economical, purposeful. Don't you know? It knows how to use what is of most value—so I, today, am led, most willingly, back to the discovery of the former me, or actually the spirits hovering over her/my head:

> In 1823 (or possibly 1824), Felix [Mendelsohn]'s maternal grandmother, Bella Salomon, presented him with a gift that was to alter the course of his life: a copyist's manuscript score of J.S. Bach's *St. Matthew Passion* . . .
>
> The score seized Felix's imagination. *Despite Bach's generally unfavorable reputation at this time (he was regarded as little more than a musical "mathematician"* [!] (a reference to what would eventually be recognized as his extraordinary use of counterpoint and musical symmetry) and the numerous difficulties presented by the score (i.e., its complexity and the unfamiliarity of its language), Felix nevertheless conceived the idea of preparing the entire *St. Matthew Passion* for performance.[7]

An "extraordinary use of counterpoint and musical symmetry"—you see, there we are again, at something ahead of its time, that needed time to be digested. And yet, Mendelsohn popped alert, just like Newton, in bed, sitting for hours, having revelations in mathematics that there was no way to prove—let the future do that—but that set us on a course of knowledge for centuries. Yes, that's the way it works. That's the key. At least till now, when "the future" pulls side by side with part of the past and says, "Hop aboard. Let's be friends. I'll speed you in advance recognition. Want to try it?" I said yes.

What would you do if you found your fingers typing things like this, as in automatic writing? I penned it down. Now it makes sense. To me, anyway, as such things will to you if they fit your narrative—bouncing back and forth through time, not satisfied with defining yourself by your physical limits. Not believing you take up only that much space. Wondering what more there is—of YOU. And then suppose something like the next text popped out, channeled through you. Who was speaking? Doesn't matter. It's You. At least, a you who popped up out of the issues of non-time, non-space, which doesn't exist either. They say.

> I am most pleased to be able to stand in myself, on the basis of this writing, as to come in on the basis of other positions or theories would not work. Thus, my birth is an implied one, in that I have a theoretical buildup, a theoretical place in which I might be located. This place did not exist, and so the purpose of the writing, in part of its intention, up to this point—a sidelight of it—was that

perhaps the end might have produced a position that could be hypothesized as perhaps the result. If the end position created such a position, it would be easy to occupy it. If not, there would be no position because one did not exist, there was not enough accumulated focus on the hypothesis— not enough life matter lived inside its question; it did not fit into Earth structures. And thus, through the creation of a personality, a place itself was permitted to exist—that is something that used to exist inside the collective unconscious, where so many of the issues were not settled, as there was not a democracy of settlement, but certain questions monopolized attention. Thus, through the uproar of the inhabitants of the Earth, asking that some of their real problems be addressed, these others, that were in the way, were taken out for problematical attack and enough attention thus given to them that it should be settled once and for all that the energy dispersed through the Earth could allow some of itself to be withdrawn from these so popular thought patterns, in order that the speeders might gather the courage and momentum to not stop at these stoplights but sail through them, go to places where, these questions already resolved, the consciousness at a further extreme was relatively practical.

So I stand, still carrying a little of the old me (or was it the new, not-yet me, waiting,

forlorn, for this me to arrive?)— Stand, watching myself write, standing on top of the energy
of the book I am now writing. I think perhaps
if I can do it, this is what I will do: for the first
time be synchronous with myself, teach others
this possibility, how, when there is no help in
the environment (not enough), when you are
blocked from proceeding further this lifetime
on the track you want to, a person, a spirit, can
draw from the self who does not exist yet, but is
waiting, NONETHELESS, very close by.

Part Two

Being

Magnetic

Letter Fragment

. . . which explained some things I didn't know I knew about magnetism. I'm sure it's quite true. I think it's an elementary, basic, primitive explanation of much that happens.

Things come together for a purpose, and purposes have magnets.

Part Three

There is no particle—there never was.

—Joseph Selbie

July 2022

Waiting for a brain MRI, I lay inside a long tube-like shape, a giant magnet. I expected a routine experience. That was not to be. My poor brain had no expectations that its job, a moment from that moment, would be *to break up alignments inside water molecules in my brain*. No. But that's what happened.

I reacted with inner horror—as my head and body felt like they were exploding. There was only one thing to do. My hand squeezed the emergency balloon. Quick. Get me out of here. Where's the exit?

This traumatic experience led me to believe the Part Two insight, just prior, even more.

To most people, it's a ho-hum matter. They do not sensitively even notice the slaughter when their brain's water cells are invaded magnetically, *the alignments broken up* to create the energy and magnetism to take medical pictures. To be more precise, as the Cleveland Clinic kindly explains, "**Magnetic resonance imaging** (MRI) works by passing an electric current through coiled wires to create a temporary magnetic field in your body—in this case, your head. A transmitter/receiver in the machine then sends and receives radio waves."

There is no "known" side effect; one assistant said to me, a little cautiously, sliding me out of the tube.

Bu then, human field "alignments," on an energetic level, are not even subject to research.

As Jef said to me later, "*Whenever I shift my perspective, my magnetic field shifts*."

The idea is, a scientific tool gets information—a brain

scan that operates through magnetism. But what about its relationship with human magnetic fields? Nonexistent? Nonsense?

Unrelated? Stay on point?

That's news to my rational brain. Doesn't magnetism of one sort affect a field of magnetism? Seems like a no-brainer Please explain it away. Tell me why my skepticism belongs off in left field. Why is the question ignorant?

But let's skip back to the supposition that *purposes have magnets*. If a particle really could make a choice that depended on wanting to make a particular choice in the future, what is going on here?

> MRIs employ powerful magnets which produce a strong magnetic field that *forces protons in the body to align with that field*. When a radiofrequency current is then pulsed through the patient, the protons are stimulated, and *spin out of equilibrium*, straining against the pull of the magnetic field.[8](emphasis added)

Out of equilibrium! If you have been paying close attention thus far, you recognize the exact principle I used to create the computer PK. Just imagine.

Back to me—squeezing the *emergency* balloon to halt the MRI in its tracks.

I could not stop myself, so huge was my sense inside the MRI tube that my body was breaking apart. Just afterwards I felt repulsion added involuntarily to my repertoire of emotions.

For a time I felt an overreaction; in those cases, I was so leery of a thing, I was, unaccountably, repelled away. And this, on the basis of a dangerous test that I only *on the off chance* needed.

Impacted by the radio waves, what happens? These aligned atoms "produce faint signals, which are used to create cross-sectional MRI images—like slices in a loaf of bread."[9]

> *During their* [MRI] *random displacements*[,] water molecules probe tissue structure at a microscopic scale . . . Sure, this story is about an apparently simple molecule, water. However, although water is an essential molecule for life, its importance in biology has perhaps been often overlooked, if not forgotten.[10] (emphasis added)

But that far-from-equilibrium state—called here "displacements"—is *the very principle* I *latched onto for the computer* PK.

I intercepted "free" energy set loose—at large—by a surge when the printer was turned on and off.

I forced it—by intercepting the normal flow of information-energy from the computer to the printer, putting the field into the briefest of *dis*equilibrium moments. Taking advantage of that instant, using that disequilibrium, I produced—voilà—the rearranged printed pages. In the induced—momentary—out-of-equilibrium state, as the energy sought a stable state, as I pushed print, then shut the computer down—giving one instruction, canceling it, giving it again (a technique that just "came to me," I don't know how—new information confiscated the programmed instruction (slipping into the "cracks," as it were), to revise it. What shifts in particles occurred in this process? Doubtless, somewhere it's a "known" tactic.

In the MRI, during "water *dis*placement," the imaging swoops in, the brain mapping occurs. But all sorts of things could capitalize on the far-from-equilibrium state; brains could. We, however, buy energy surge protectors! Do not know how to use the surge of energy. Heaven forbid.

Heaven does nothing of the sort. It made this energy available to us.

Technology once again is going ahead, as we humans, looking neither right nor left, do not notice this amazing opening we could walk into, this energy available—to us we pass on to just machines.

> On the scale of the solar system, with planets
> far apart, gravity is much more important than
> magnetism.[11]

Be that all as it may, let's go back to "Things come together for a purpose, and purposes have magnets."

What if intent directs energy—and it does? Imagine what adding the magnet of purpose to it brings.

> In the "gaping hole" where light and mat-
> ter behave as now a particle, now a wave, "it
> became increasingly clear that light or matter
> only behaves like particles in the presence of an

intelligent observer . . . The discovery left physicists feeling they had joined the Mad Hatter's
tea party.[12]"

In particle colliders, detectors "sensitive to high-energy
radiation and electrodynamic energy" capture the collisions:

These detectors provide spectacular images of
what looks to the uneducated eye like an explosion. What the detectors detect are quanta
(energy packets) hitting the detectors in the
instants after the collision.

It's fair, then, to ask, Are those quanta
emitted from a particle or from a vibration of a
field? At the instant of collision, did a particle
momentarily become formless energy and then
reform as another type of particle, or was it
energy all along? And does it make any differ-
ence? The answer to the last question is: Not
really. Einstein's discovery of the equivalence
of matter and energy renders the question
irrelevant.

As I mentioned previously, "particles" called
bosons, specifically photons and gluons, have
no mass at all. Even particles *with* mass, such
as quarks, have their mass quantified as the
electron volts of *energy* they contain. The desire
to classify the subatomic realm in terms of particles is purely a reflection of the way we think

about the everyday world as our senses reveal it. We deal with discrete objects. We pick up a glass We throw a ball. We clean a fork. We are predisposed to visualize the subatomic realm in a similar way—but it simply isn't similar.[13]

Hover over these concluding sentence and let them float around inside you. Let them tell you what they mean: particles are not discrete, distinct, with a physical shape, etc., that gives them identity. Like us. No, what identifies, quantifies, a particle, if it has mass at all, is *the electron volts* of its energy.

Dogs and other animals lacking our ability to "think it through"—some of them do get their most important information about us from our energy. With a hop and a skip, we jumped over this option in evolution. And kept jumping. We still are. Till now we meet technology. And what? We transfer the potential to *its* world. We don't need to learn those skills. Do we? All agreed, say yes.

Meanwhile, "Your brain is made of approximately 100 billion nerve cells, called neurons . . .the electrochemical aspect lets them transmit signals over long distances (up to several feet or a few meters) and send messages to each other."[14]

So our brain is busy transmitting signals, some we want it to. Some, we know nothing about.

A 3 T MRI scanner is around 60,000 times stronger than the earth's magnetic field![15]

No matter. I'm immune. Bring it on.

Part Four

Fields, Apologies, Tricks High Up

A respectable theory, explains *The Physics of God* (by Joseph Selbie), states that matter is nothing but *"energies in a stable vibrating equilibrium,"* but beyond that is a theory that "a particle is really just an *excited* state of an underlying *field."* This is field theory (FT),

> but it becomes known as quantum field the-
> ory (QFT) when the behavior of such fields is
> considered at the subatomic level. Instead of
> having to visualize a collided particle vaporizing
> into an unstable fog of energy and then recon-
> densing into a new and stable form, imagine
> instead that there is no particle—there never
> was; instead, the added energies have caused
> new excitations at different points in a field.[16]

To return to this topic I *barely* dipped into elsewhere, QFT, it "treats particles as excited states (also called quanta) of their underlying quantum fields, which are more fundamental than the particles."[17]

What? Excited states . . . more fundamental than particles? The "excited me" is more "real"? Hmm. Reflect a moment. The "excited me" is *as* real as—at least—the nonexcited me, the "excited me" jumping into the interstices, taking me by surprise. Or, at least, it stands out in the field identifiably, in a different "position"? This paragraph "jumped into" me and is here for pondering.

No wonder we place such high stakes on intensity. Is that when we "exist'? when we get into an excited state as the excited particles ripple their energy up to us? And we catch them. We live it. Is that it?

"The current theoretical understanding of the fundamental interactions of matter is based on quantum field theories of [the various] forces."[18]

So, once again, now that we know what some quantum physicists think about it, let's go back to the description of the MRI I endured as I got "zapped.":

Excited protons—fundamentally, fields—"spun out of equilibrium" in me as a radio frequency "pulsed" through me after powerful magnets "force[d] protons in the body to align with that field" it set up. OK, got it.

Pictures of my brain got snapped. Medically helpful. And life went on as normal. See, no harm done.

At least, that was the prediction, but not for me.

Even a month later, I remained traumatized—the same as how the whole Earth would respond if a stream of comets came too close into its atmosphere.

Imagine the cells fighting for their life, the water cells being torn from a beautiful crystal shape into disarray.

A Few Months Later

Apologies to everyone I convinced with my interpretation. To all sympathizers.

New information has reached me that says my explanation was entirely false. At least, not complex enough. All the while that I was pushing the emergency balloon, in total, abject shock and dismay, affronted to my core, what was happening if we could peek in elsewhere? And we can.

Well, not at all what I just described!

Crafty me, I *did not resist the magnet*! Beneath my own knowledge (knowing I would doubtless find out), I did something else entirely. That is, on a very high level, outside the scope of what my consciousness, on the human level, down here as "me," could follow. Or knew was possible.

Weeks later, trying to reassemble my shredded energy, I contacted Mariah Martin, of Light Enterprises. I used to contact her regularly but we had not touched base for years. A beautiful Light worker and psychic.

She set my interpretation on its head. What happened was A Field Meeting a Field, by her description. What happens then? Well, it can capture the energy in it. Use it.

Like a giant being intercepting a spacecraft, able to poise it on a powerful finger and steer it to a desired location, some higher energy I was associated with had taken the energy over.

What?

Like standing as an observer at the Jornada del Muerto, near Los Alamos, when the experimental first nuclear bomb was exploded—deciding not to just look but to take the energy as a throttle thrust—this high-energy-prone, high-energy-comfortable part of me leapt on for the ride. Realized it was, personally speaking, *a rare concentration of energy that didn't come my way often. For what? To travel on!!!*

No sane person would even think of jumping into the MRI force field. This went on beyond my conscious mind, like so much that happens to us until we investigate, *track down the invisible biography of our life.*

"I" knew nothing about it, remember.

Under the "computer-PK" principle—by which super-charged energy becomes available when an electrical system is *disrupted*—some part of me <u>able to do</u> so climbed aboard—maybe clamored, as likely this was a multiple-entity operation?—recognizing the energy freed up in the surge. As if hanging onto a jet plane taking off, this higher energy, equal to the task, used the energy, not letting go of the "wing" as the jet propulsion geared up and the plane was aloft,.

Now, lowly me, physically on the table, inside the magnetic tunnel—remember, though, I too am a field according to the above *Physics of God* explanations—had no indication of this except by what it felt like. Bang. Spatters of me about to spread over the table in all directions. Have you ever felt the energy build till you knew you would explode at the next second? I never had. I now have.

It precipitated an initiation. I have become used to them. They always take me by surprise; there hadn't been one for some time.

This time, I did not even realize I had gone *way out beyond my consciousness* (that is, the one typing here).

I arrived back in my body, feeling around at the chunks of "me" debris. Arrived back in the room, outside the tube, *with no idea that I had been warp-sped into some unlogged experience.*

The question is, how to assimilate what I didn't even know had happened, like in a near-death experience where the memory is gone but returns thereafter in snatches? Well, I had help. Let me tell you. Also, I needed to find out myself what space had opened up

Why did my super-consciousness—or super-consciousness itself or the surrounding spirit field—take me off on an initiation into energy previously unexplored by me? beyond my abilities to comprehend? Evidently, the wildly intense magnetic energy was irresistible. Seeing the ideal launch pad, I was turned into a rocket. Looked at from beyond the Earth energies, it supplied just that force needed to send me, as it were, into orbit. And back.

Earth, feel the plug
as it goes into you,
of the universe.

The electrical field, expanded into.
Now plugged in, not just to the galaxy, but to
    All time
    One time
    Once in a lifetime
    You

Editor's Note

It took a while to realize what had changed in the enduring aftereffect. But there definitely was one.

"Equal and opposite" to the impact, the cause, the change was that I realized *the energy of the higher me was now looming closer* to the surface of the Earth, with a propulsion strong enough to reach me forcibly. Surreptitiously, easily (no bumps), I came upon the fact that I *from thereon more and more believed myself.* Well. Doesn't everyone? Absolutely not. That's another thing we are here on Earth to do.

Long story short: the life I had lived for ten years in the 1990s, that retracted further and further from me as the twenty-first century brought its own interests (and distractions) now returned to *a sense of reality*, but different. Now the messages I had excitedly, dutifully, written every day back then, so new, coming from somewhere else, *gained believability.* I took my version of Pascal's wager.

This time, when the Great Questioner came around, asking, "Who do you believe, the outer investigators and truth establishers or yourself?" it was as if I couldn't afford to straddle the fence. The messages gained reality, yes. *But coming from myself. Not an outer spirit group, though there was that. But the thoughts were now mine. I could identify with me.*

I didn't really stop to think what had happened. The energy to do so arrived innocuously. Unannounced.

But asking myself the question now, observing myself from inside and out, I realize that I am much more all of a piece. I was *forced to choose*, evidently. Choose which me to go

46

on with. In fact, choosing the one meant life, I didn't know. But chose it.

Choosing the other meant I needed an overhaul; had become too "infected" with Earth belief systems; was "hopeless," as it were, if to go further into this lifetime with the promise of it. After all, I had done a lot. To go further, I had to *jump aboard this me*, the one I had "talked to" in the '90s.

It happened effortlessly. I barely noticed the change.

In other words, I put aside *all* worries about my health, even threatened with a life-threatening disease. No, my focus of attention was *not* to make one last trip—supposing it proved to be that—not to tell someone I loved her (or him). All that seemed taken care of. What remained to be done was go back into the '90s. Find the *living material* from there—kicking with energy—that was entrusted to me.

That I had put into boxes *and preserved*. But, as I've said elsewhere, to act like that would only have worked in an earlier century. Once, in the 1990s, a Hindu guru told me I was not synchronized with myself in this time period—that energetically my public self did not exist in the contemporary time frame. It existed in a future time frame.

I had not whipped myself into shape, consciousness wise.

Let him reorganize me energetically, he offered.

I was aghast. No, I told him, *he couldn't work in my energy*. No. But I took that idea from him. Now, in 2022, I had to do it myself. Twirl myself around and let the loose ends either leave or be tied up. And not in a knot. No, in a bow for 2022. 2023. So I plunged in. All my energies were pulled upward. Creativity took over. I had no thoughts for anything else.

Healing invariably occurred. Healing energies will align with this outlook, I discovered. And they give the spilling-over energy back to you (to me) in large doses.

Look and see if something like this is also being presented to you. Does it offer a possible explanation to unusual experiences or an extreme situation you might find yourself in? Would this explanation make sense? Give you fighting power or "belief" power? Try it out. That is, are you being given the chance to go to another level, maybe even much higher, or much much higher? Are you being asked to, at least, believe yourself???

Letter in the 1990s to a friend

The question of work has come in so strongly because there is a contract finished, through that could not be perceived; the perception is being forced onto me but not precisely the solution, except in the Knowing realm. But that realm is asking my personality level realm, where the personality no longer existed, how it will respond, now that the needs have shifted. Can it walk into the

[carpenters. Mt. 13:55]

Is not this the carpenter, the son of Mary, the brother of James, and Joses, and Juda? And are not his sisters here with us? And they were offended at him.
Mark 5: But Jesus said unto them, "A prophet is not without honor, but in his own country, and among his own kin, and in his own house."

existence, but under orders that had a future that required a different structure? And that's

[Gleaning]

1597Xa big question to

[Holiness. Of God]

confront. It's the next spiral, where many are not even to the point of realizing that spiral is here. What I do is hold up a standard, and whoever is attracted to the standard has just as

*2066Xmuch

[Prophets.
Names of persons spoken of as]

a right to the space as I. And yet, we haven't fig-
ured out these issues yet. And so here I stand.

I have done my job. I have a new job coming
in. And yet the continuation of my first job contract is too important to me to just drop. I have
set things up for this second contract. I would
like to supervise it. But I also need a higher-ca-
pacity energy container or form that knows how
to walk through the omega-alpha nondeath
position. And only in those moments, wherever
they occur and over and over, will the Cross
really be stepped off of in the highest honor
with ten-gun salutes. So the energy of

and I am not so much located in a human form in those moments, and I have therefore decided to let the personality level re-form and not question its position as recipient of information it normally should not have but must have, for it is its new self in active re-transformation . . . And in giving everything encounter the understanding of those who know how to *receive everything and not take it as theirs. So my personality is learning to exist and not exist at the same time as one born and not born, and try to imagine the shape that looks like.* I am trying not to take from anyone, as that would be my own essence that was taken from me, but also to understand how to create the place that the Intention is creating. In all humility.

2022

So spake that me. The one of the 1990s. Not Zarathustra, but perhaps A Book for All and None. What happened next?

I moved back to the United States—barely ten days before 9/11, by chance. But that's neither here nor there to this story.

Suffice it to say, I did get my container of furniture and these papers delivered just beforehand.

Departing from Belgium did not mean leaving forever the splash caused in me by that ten years of channeling, when the rocket ships landed down on Earth in far-off waters without so much as a TV anchor on hand to report. No, I was supposed to bring these materials to light, and there was no getting out of it. Not that I wanted to, but I didn't know how. And now, albeit with the gun of a medical scare at my back, I have picked those drafts up. Pages and pages, manuscript after manuscript. Yes, there are several of them.

Well, as my old friend Milton Klonsky often reminded me, "When the time comes to finish, you . . .

". . . JUST FINISH."

✳

I honed in on the 1990s words "I have done my job. I have a new job coming in." They reach me now from decades past: "done my job." I had. Then. But they reach me as if buried in a time warp. Were they? Dipping into *that* mind, from back then, I *find the exact questions* I *ponder now*. A resonating voice ejects itself from *that* energy and approaches.

Looking for support anywhere, some clue, I *find it here.* Someone who understands my position now.

Mesmerized by the words from the "past," I think how they apply today. Now, it's as if every word is cut out of *my* urgent search for answers. As if the same situation had come back round. My consciousness is ready. I don't think it was then.

As if the veil of time lifted, and in the 1990s I was knowingly speaking to this living, present, then-future me now, and vice versa. Now I am knowingly, directly, listening to that me then. Uncannily, I find there answers this 2022 me is searching for.

That me, guided word for word as to what to tell me! What applies.

✖

To set this up, let's sit with Charles Lindberg as he crosses the Atlantic. It is 1927, as deliciously brought to life in Break *through the Limits of the Brain.*

Incredibly tired after weeks of preparation and last-minute badgering by reporters, he had thirty-three and a half hours to Paris ahead of him in which he had to stay awake every second. But a few hours after takeoff his eyes felt like "salted stones." As the narrator, Charles Selbie, tells us, the sleep-deprived Lindbergh "could not allow himself to lift either of his feet from the rudder controls or to take both hands from the stick," much less close his eyes. In this state, where there was a lack of modern automatic controls, the responsibility fell squarely in his lap. And suddenly, midflight, he broke through into a state of super-concentration—thus avoiding dosing off: "There's no limit to my sight—my skull is one great eye, seeing everywhere at once . . . All sense of substance leaves. There's no longer weight to my body, no longer hardness to the stick. The feeling of flesh is gone. I become independent of physical laws . . . Will I become a consciousness in space, all-seeing, all-knowing, unhampered by materialistic fetters of the world?"[19]

In that way, he finished his round-the-world flight.

✳

It was seven hours into the first chemo session. It was just ending. Seven hours. But I felt like booking a room, things had gone so well. Truly, what with the anti-anxiety meds in the IV. Besides which, I had a positive outlook.

But where was my iPad?

I was not startled, but it had disappeared. There in the chemo room.

I was fascinated, curious. Why? When putting on the ice-pack gloves to protect my hands from the drugs, I'd slipped the laptop behind my back in my chair. It wasn't there. The nurses began a search.

Well, could it possibly have been swept up in removing my blanket?

More staff arrived, shaking every dirty blanket in the laundry. Not there. Definitely. One nurse lamented, "I don't know what to do."

I left, still "giddy" from the meds—carrying my Harry Potter light stick invisibly in my hand.

There are many "questionable" disappearances, but very few are *undeniable*. To be that, a thing has to physically vanish *and then reappear in a new location*, as clear as day—as happened in the two events below. I do not consider the disappearing laptop an unquestionable disappearance. This leads me to another tale. It's from a manuscript I put aside: *Things That Disappear*.

In my bathroom in Tienen, Belgium, I was putting clothes into my mini-Swiss washing machine one early evening. The mini machine had a spinning cylinder in the center, a narrow space between it and the side of the machine. Dangling dangerously off my eyes, my glasses fell in. Into the narrow space—too small for my hand. Irrefutably, they left my eyes and fell between the cylinder and outer edge of the machine.

There was absolutely no way to reach in and get them out. Maybe some handyman could drop a tool down through the slit. But not tonight.

Waking the next morning, I went sleepily into the living room, bypassing the bathroom. Oops, what was that I almost stepped on? Don't be skeptical. Or, yes, it's your prerogative, as you weren't there at my side. But fortunately, I looked down to where my foot was about to step. What lay there? My glasses.

I suppose they acquired legs that could walk them out of one tight jam into the next room? No, of course not. No, *how*? you ask. And I ask. What could cause inanimate objects—but that, mind you, are made of particles—to relocate room to room?

Incontrovertibly, in the morning my eyeglasses lay on the floor in front of me, and the night before, inconvertibly, were trapped in the machine—facts that did not mesh.

56

Of course, such an experience did not happen often. Only twice to me in this obvious a fashion.

Years passed. One day in Raleigh, North Carolina, I changed into street clothes in the—by coincidence—*bathroom. I had just finished a ballet class.*

As I was dressing in the bathroom, I was otherwise ready to leave. Except, where were *my ballet shoes? Ballet shoes don't hide. I canvassed the tiny room.* Nothing. I was sure, but eyes are tricky. The brain is.

Seeing someone in the lobby, I asked for help. I did not tell her my suspicion. We searched inch by inch—nothing. Now, my rational mind knew the shoes were *not in the bathroom.* Impossible, or not, they simply were not there,

I finally gave up and went to the car, opened the door, and—you guessed it? Perched like Dorothy's red shoes in *The Wizard of Oz,* there they were Those battered pink ballet slippers. *On the passenger seat.* Now, no, I didn't have two pairs. They sat there as if the ballet class had been erased and, with time wound backwards, I was just about to start class, not leave it—as if rolling up time like a rug you could then unroll at will. I challenge you to find an explanation.

> I'm on the border line of life and a greater realm beyond, as though caught in the field of gravitation between two planets, acted on by forces I can't control, forces too weak to be measured by any means at my command, yet representing powers incomparably stronger than I've ever known.
>
> —Lindbergh

Beneath matter's seeming fluidity is a fluid dance of energy. Matter's essential fluidity gives us the first hint of how miracles and other phenomena, such as telekinesis, can occur.

—Seife

Ah-ha. So it makes sense. How, prey tell? What does he make of this hint?

> That matter results from the invisible organization of energy suggests the possibility that this invisible organization can be changed. Matter is not rigid; it is not a permanently unchanging thing.[20]

So there you have it.

Possibly possible, Seife speculates above, through reaching into the "invisible organization of energy," invisible because we see only the tiniest bit, perhaps 10 percent, of physical reality. But beyond where we see, it is organized. Ah-ha. Voilà. Work in the organization. Ah-ha.

❋

THINGS THAT DISAPPEARED
AND RETURNED BUT AMBIGUOUSLY

I knew I was being "decloaked." The parts of me on my higher levels, which I was not for a long time skilled enough to even speak about, had been—as a Big Dream about nineteen years earlier explained—given a way to appear on the Earth *if I learned how to speak of them from the bottom up; that is, from the most everyday level of conversation, naturally.* At that time, I stood on a high-up plateau, but, the dream indicated, only my intuition could "follow" me up there; I had no skill to communicate at so abstract a height, before things beamed themselves down into events here—when, up there without physical form and histories, they were merely ideas and "truths."

So I was "put under a fountain"; that way another aspect of me—formerly grossly neglected by me—would become my "mouthpiece." After, that is, it was cleared of its many many issues; that period was now over; that ignored part—no longer awkward socially—now represented me in public: my unskilled, extraverted, people-oriented self now confident, no matter where, I listened to her as she zoomed out of the unconscious, bringing what she knew from having been there so long.

Left outside "me," she'd risked being gnawed by "wild animals" (unconscious vulnerabilities, patterns) or becoming malformed, being tied in knots in lack of self-confidence. Again, that didn't happen. She'd merely been isolated, left unevolved, deprived of association with me, as I lived—ignorant of my need for this part of me, these skills—on the high-up plateau. That is, in my intuition.

My *down-on-the-ground personality now had a place in me*—my intuition having reached a dead end, insofar as going public, in not having mastered communication skills without it. Arriving at that dream plateau outside La Sagrada Familia (the Holy Family) Basilica of Barcelona, I (the intuition) was to be preempted of my governing role, demoted, *or rather fused*. That was in 1985. It took time. But so it was. And is. Fusion accomplished.

I discovered (over the intervening years) that I had marvelous latent communication skills. I just hadn't looked inside to where the undeveloped gift was lying, dirty, homeless.

So, what was the purpose of the whisked-away iPad in 2022? For one thing, I call it the universe "acting out" a situation.

Here, it beautifully, playfully, messaged to me, speaking a language I understand:

> See. Your mini dachshund Hans "disappeared yesterday." You had to send him to doggie heaven. He's with us. He's fine. He's with St. Francis. He's with your prior dachshund Snoepie. And Snoep. Well, we won't tell you exactly where he is. But the pet communicator who sent him Reiki remote while he was being given the medicine to "sleep" reported that *he was flown, in excitement, by a pilot to the steps of a great pyramid-like structure, ran up the steps, and disappeared into a Great Light.* Your cancer is disappearing. We've got this. We're in charge here.

OK. Much better than if I'm in charge. Let's see where this is going. *Oh, sticky note: Don't forget to tell the cells.*

How does science see gravity? If space-time is a dimension that *"form[s] a malleable fabric that is distorted by matter,"* what's the hitch?

> *Physicists struggling to reconcile gravity with quantum mechanics have hailed a theory—inspired by pencil lead—that could make it all very simple.*

It was a speech that changed the way we think of space and time. The year was 1908, and the German mathematician Hermann Minkowski had been trying to make sense of Albert Einstein's hot new idea—what we now know as special relativity—describing how things shrink as they move faster and time becomes distorted. "Henceforth space by itself and time by itself are doomed to fade into the mere shadows," Minkowski proclaimed, "and only a union of the two will preserve an independent reality."

And so space-time—the malleable fabric whose geometry can be changed by the gravity of stars, planets and matter—was born. It is a concept that has served us well, but if physicist Petr Horava is right, it may be no more than a mirage. Horava, who is at the University of California, Berkeley, wants to rip this fabric apart and set time and space *free from one another* in order to come up with a unified theory that reconciles the disparate worlds of quantum mechanics and gravity—one the most pressing challenges to modern physics.[21] (my italics)

What did Einstein have to say about the intersection of time and space? We all know the basics:

Time and space, according to Einstein's theories of relativity, are woven together, forming

a four-dimensional fabric called "space-time."
The mass of Earth dimples this fabric, much
like a heavy person sitting in the middle of a
trampoline. Gravity, says Einstein, is simply
the motion of objects following the curvaceous
lines of the dimple.

(This theory of general relativity was just confirmed in
Gravity Probe B, NASA *reported in* 2011.)

If Earth were stationary, that would be the
end of the story. But Earth is not stationary.
Our planet spins, and the spin should twist
the dimple, slightly, pulling it around into a
4-dimensional swirl.[22]

That's clear. And then it wasn't.

A LONG time ago, in a galaxy far away, two
black holes collided. We know this because
more than a billion years later, on the morning
of 14 September 2015, we felt it: in the world's
most exquisitely sensitive measuring device,
laser beams shifted ever so slightly as ripples
in space-time washed over Earth.

The first detection of gravitational waves
was the culmination of an epic scientific quest,
and a stunning endorsement of general relativity, Einstein's landmark theory of gravity. Since

then, our detectors have seen them five more times. But this is just the start—and although everything we have learned from the first waves is consistent with Einstein's masterpiece, the coming deluge of sightings could tear it apart.

Gravitational waves carry us into uncharted waters, where the fabric of the universe is so warped and gravity so extreme that our best theories are pushed to their limits . . .

As engineers recalibrate the lasers to make the detectors yet more sensitive, physicists are buzzing with anticipation about what they might reveal. Theorists are now entertaining cosmic oddities that could transform our understanding of black holes, gravity, and space-time itself.[23]

And, a piece of me asks, inquiringly, what about when things "act themselves out"?—that is, based on meaning, they communicate "a message" by acting it out.

And are "Things That Disappear" likewise Acted-Out messages—at least often? A subcategory of the universe's practice of communicating visually. *For thoughts speak; they know how to. But there is a type of communication that does not speak, its expression often being kinetic—in motion, and motion makes a picture.*

That is, nature or anything or anyone can bring us information by pinpointing a coincidental timing. How did I put that earlier, in a retrieved page? Ah, here it is:

So many things I
DO NOT KNOW.

I do not know precisely why the images I see
there are in the sky—the mind impressions, it
seems—and whose they are (are they anyone's?),
where they came from. I DO KNOW they are beautiful and take focused concentration to see and in
being seem, come nearer and in more focus.

The "one who thought" had the power of
speech. The "one who did not know through
thought" did not have the power of speech.
It was as if existing in thin air, to the thinker.
There was nothing to grasp of its reasons, its
proofs. They even might change and not be
there any more by the time they were searched
for—or the very next second. They might comer
complete and last forever with no proof of ever
having been. Or they might come in a form that
had to be worked on and stayed. And was even-
tually clearly there.

The form of proof that the believer
ha+3333666662d, the one subsisting in knowing, was that that had learned something (or
realized it knew something) in the form that
Plato called remembering. Somewhere within
itself it had the power TO KNOW.

But if you did not exist, you could not
remember. How could you say, "I know because

I have remembered" if you did not exist? And there was no proof it was you that was the rememberer?

Was there any proof that it was you that had the doubt? You that thought?

DESCARTES KNEW HE THOUGHT. He was proving it through the line of thinking called knowing.

Descartes put his finger on the pulse of the age at that time. It was sure it existed and sure it thought. Ergo, it was in the spirit of the time to be sure that existence was to be found through the understanding of the thinking mind. The mind that thought, it was the one asking for development. It was its turn. It was the times that called forth, through the collective unconscious, development of the thinker.

We already knew logic. Now we could develop the logic. We could make a tool of it. We could begin our stockhouse of mental tools.

Back to the universe's practice of communicating visually. I was walking my little dog, Hans. Uncharacteristically as had never before happened, an animal sprang suddenly out of the bushes—in an "excited state"—as if to put Hans at risk. In the suddenness, the emotion, the gasp it drew from me, another event, soon to-be, leaped into my thoughts. Instantaneously.

Hans was imminently going to be in boarding at the vet's. But he was weak, with kidney disease. I associated some totally unexpected sudden danger was "in the field." My mind just put the two side by side. An alert. I took measures.

Had the event happened in other circumstances, it would have carried no meaning for me, but I felt it like "messenger" hormones in the body, transplanted into the universe or vice-versa, bringing me information yet again, in this usually dismissed, fashion—not in our book of languages.

Or wait! Yes, I see it clearly now—it was yet again an example of what can happen in that disruptive, dissipative, in-between disequilibrium state. Defining "dissipative system," Wikipedia says:

> A dissipative system is a **thermodynamically open system** which is operating out of, and often far from, thermodynamic equilibrium in an environment with which it exchanges energy and matter. A tornado may be thought of as a dissipative system. Dissipative systems stand in contrast to conservative systems.

Catching me off guard, it allowed just an instant in which normal thought was replaced by a tone of warning—was pushed aside in this second of surprise, of disequilibrium.

"Symbolic actions"—visual consciousness—which I have long believed in, slipped in. I noticed it out of the corner of my eye. It was the computer-PK principle out there on my walk.

We are the warps in space.
Everything with mass does it. An emotion? A thought? *Warps in space.*
Who I am, truly, warps space. It does?

That popped in from Nowhere—this morning.

> For example, a pencil will create its own grav-
> itational field, *but the gravitational pull will be so*
> *miniscule and small that it simply could not be detected*
> *with modern technology.*[24] (my emphasis)

Even a pencil does it. Energy meets US—and—what? dis-
regards its "content"? Why would it? What if it does not?
I am being hand-fed these little phrases.
Relative position is energy. Contours of objects together are.
And now the cells. They too have a universe where, if
we don't talk to them, don't include the plant life, don't
include mechanical progress as part of consciousness, we
will be—as we enlarge our information pools—decreasing
our consciousness breadth. We will be writing ourselves
out of history. Oh no.

Then this:

I was watching kids at an amusement park, 2022. I thought:
What if, years from now, people will look back at us and realize that all
that focus on Covid was part of the cause? that—

Thoughts are carriers of disease!

Wait, hold it. How many decades, centuries did you jump ahead?

Well, I add it to the "it just popped ins"—a fact that was residing somewhere on the other side of our reality. If focus creates attraction, if observation *influences* what it observes, then doesn't the thought *carrying* the focus—as photons carry electromagnetism—carry the attraction as well? Or can? Focus on peace attracts peace. Fear begets fear.

Why didn't we add the facts up to get the right approach to attraction in the sense of a dimension, a facet, of gravity?

※

I addressed the spirit world: *What happened to me in the* MRI? Where did I go, while lying, helpless, in the dark?

And perfectly timed as it weighed on my mind, I sat down for a Zoom meet (prescheduled) with shaman, master Taiji teacher, Taoist Jef Crab. A private chat, which always gets deep. And wouldn't you know? I brought up the MRI, thinking idly perhaps he'd have a comment. He was full of information. I quote extracts a few pages ahead. In fact, the explanations and observations are rich enough that I put it in full on my website.

Part Five

The CLUE the MRI Gave Me

Conversation with Jef Crab—August 12, 2023
Deep into Explanations of the MRI Demolishing Me

JC: The personality has to be shattered in order to enter this level [the quantum state] . . . You have to leave your personality behind . . . in a conscious way.

MAH: So you have to know you're leaving your personality behind. OK. That makes sense. This is very interesting too . . . You would think that "dropping the body" in Mahasamadhi, that is, where you're not coming back—would you think that involved entering the quantum state?

JC: Yes, Mahasamadhi is that state. One step higher. But it's not entering or re-entering. It's whether you choose to enter that state. You can choose to remain in your body or choose to leave your body.

MAH: But in Mahasamadhi you're leaving the body. So you're entering that state as your pure awareness. You would say you're entering a higher state than the particle mind? The God-conscious mind?

JC: I'll try to describe what I experience. We have a word for it in Dutch. It's called Full/Empty. Beyond multidimensionality there's a state of being. It's called Full/Empty. It's the opposites, which are one. The yin/yang go back to the primordial state. It's something before manifestation.

Beyond multidimensionality it's where yin and yang come back to the primordial state. It's something before manifestation. It's full bright light and complete darkness at the same time. It's full Movement and stillness at the same time.

MAH: Like the Shiva statue . . . I've been into pure awareness many times, but it was not like smashing your body. So it's not pure awareness . . . it's something before manifestation.

JC: No, it's pure awareness in the manifestation Whenever mind will manifest itself, it will manifest itself through an infinite number of possibilities. Is that correct?

MAH: Yes.

JC: OK. By coming down, the oneness shatters itself. Well, when most people go through this, they just come down to the ordinary personality in order to come down to themselves on a lower level. They are binding together like an onion in order to become themselves on a lower level.

This is in between. Most people just skip this state of infinite possibility in a conscious state. By going up, we can enter this level of infinite possibilities in a conscious way— seeing a person healed before even connecting to it. From being in this state and accepting this as the most primal experience. Seeing the person in his true capacity. . .

MAH: Quite interesting, the way you describe it . . . I will take that with me because I have been in the void, or pure awareness, but I think you're talking about adding something to it, which must be a different level, like the pure void void.

JC: It is the same experience. I'll try to explain something I experience, which is similar to what you experienced in the MRI by this magnetic field shattering your personality . . . because personality is a magnetic field. I think we agree on that. My attitude this moment is defined by my magnetic field. I'm 100 percent sure of this. The moment I change my attitude in a certain situation or not a situation, my electromagnetic field changes . . . This can also happen by entering the MRI probably. In shamanism . . . we distinguish this episode. We could never claim that we shamans create the beneficial circumstances. We don't wait . . . we *search* for the beneficial circumstances . . . If they didn't exist, we wouldn't be able to do it.

I am not the one who decides, though. I can reject the circumstance. I cannot create them. Creating them is something much higher. On the level of the creative forces, maybe.

When we enter this pure mind level, in order to manifest these beneficial circumstances for ourselves or others, I think it's similar to what you described.

MAH: *Oh, yeah.*

JC: In the beginning, it seems to the personality—*my mind is exploding.* After a while you don't need to go through this. The pure mind will shatter the personality . . . I don't like to talk about higher or lower . . . At a certain moment it has to be shattered to bring the personality into this state.

MAH: That's amazing.

MAH: If I had asked you when this happened, it wouldn't have helped. I was really shattered and I needed help to bring the pieces together again . . . for my makeover.

[JC suggests going back to that state and examining it.] There's no problem in re-membering, becoming part of it again.

MAH: That's a good suggestion: that I go back to that state. Ask: *What is doing the shattering. What is beyond the shattering?*

JC: I suggest that you only go back to the shattering and *observe* . . . I'm convinced of the unity of all living beings, and it's a natural process.

MAH: This process that you are describing began for me in 1994, when I was studying with you. And when Dhyanyogi-ji was about to drop the body. So in 1994 I didn't tell people, but my back went into a collapse; I had a block—mysteriously— and I would have to roll over slowly to figure out how I could get out of bed. And I had to get weekly traction. I knew it was mysterious, some kind of energy thing.

    While this was going on, I would lie in bed with my eyes closed, and I would enter this awareness. I was walking, with nothing around me. Just dark. It was not positive or negative. It was just dark, and I would experience this state, which would be dark, and I knew if I kept going I would be gone from my body and never get back. I didn't know why this was happening, so I would just lie there and experience this state of walking, the awareness, with the awareness that to go much further, there would be no way back into my body . . . You know, an awareness, you identify with it. . . it would just come. And then Dhyanyogi-ji left the body, and Jyoti told me maybe a year later that he spent the whole last year of his life in bed. And suddenly it came together for me: that was his awareness. *And that he was walking into samadhi beforehand. And somehow I got into his awareness. I was walking in the awareness.* I don't tell people this.

And when my light body co-founder left the body, this came to me, that he was following the path of leaving the body consciously.

Anyway, I got all these pieces. They made much different sense when I followed them back to 1994, Dhyanyogi-ji. And how I got there, I don't know. But there was no explosion.

JC: You know, beyond the fourth level, in shamanism—of course, everybody has their own system to experience these levels . . . So beyond going through the primordial sound, which is completely light, the first hours after the decease . . .

MAH: Perhaps it was beyond the explosion.

JC: In Buddhism there is this primordial light. They say in the beginning, in the first hours after the death, there will be this primordial light, and you have to jump into it . . . Beyond that it is light and it is dark. It is the brightest light and the deepest dark at the same time. In my experience, this is actually the state of mind; this deep darkness is affecting everything. It is imminent. There is no manifestation yet. It is possible to reach this level during our life. Especially in samadhi. In deep mediation we can enter this level, where there is nothing to do, nothing to see. It's beyond existence. There are no words for it. It's impossible to describe it. It connects to what you are describing.

It connects to an experience I had in the '80s. I went to see the Dalai Lama. On the third occasion he just looked me in the eyes, and everything became this deep deep deep black. He literally turned back and looked me in the eyes, and it was shakti. I thought it was a blackout. Later I understood that by entering this level, I could enter this vibration again.

[Jef said that the first time he saw the Dalai Lama he became aware of a vibration.]

It was strong and it was light, and I said: *This is something I will have to achieve in this life as well.* But the third time I saw him, he looked me in the eyes, and it was exactly what you describe: it was this deep black level.

MAH: That is all so amazing. You know, Dhyanyogi-ji, the Dalai Lama—they exist on these levels, these planes. It's not like something we're taught in school, that they even exist. It's mystical, I guess you say.

JC: Yes.

ME [after a bit] There is nothing I can say that you don't have an experience about.

JEF: because I'm not an educated person. He tells the story of the spiritual teacher in India who said, "I'm not an educated person. It's hard to stay uneducated." The spiritual teacher was answering a question about how he knew so much. "Not being an educated person, I remember my experiences," he said. And Jef said. And I say.

I asked Jef to read my next book in manuscript but added that I was apprehensive, a bit, because I opened up about my vulnerabilities at that earlier age.

Jef said to never be afraid to communicate your experiences. "Because it is my firm belief communicating is the only thing we can pass on." He explained that for this reason he revealed, "This is what Joska [Soos] did to me. This is what the Dalai Lama did to me.

"That way, people can experience with me. It's experiences that make us grow. They are a primary source of *knowledge*. Not information . . .

> However we shiver in the sight of the divine, it's still a humane experience, and it remains a humane experience, and it's not strange to humanity. Never be afraid to communicate it . . . That's why we're here.

✻

Now having abandoned the practice of saying I made the whole thing up, I'm quite at home vouching for the integrity, the reality, of all my experiences. I changed 180 degrees. A*nd*

people began to listen. I did not make it up! All my experiences have, even, an explanation with scientific weight. It has to do with the fact that invisible energy is organized—invisibly. A consensus emerges. Oops. Not yet. But not far off, this new recognition of yet one more aspect of human potential pushed under a stone we did not turn over. And then we did.

I reject the opening of this book. I present the extraordinary experiences as fact.

Matter-of-factly, a matter of course. I do not make a big deal of it. But I am grateful to them for all the friends they turned up, the joyful wonder of being in front of Mystery. The astonishment at the Universe, at what it gives us to experience if we choose. I am grateful. I acknowledge the Universe. The spirit guides in it. The experiences themselves, from wherever they came. I bow down to how divine it all is. We are. You are.

✻

Months passed. More layers unpeeled. So high up I had not even sensed they were there. I felt sure my "explosion," gathering an explanation that it was a method of entering The Light, had shown its transpersonal face. Yes, yes. That's it. I felt my heart swell. A path OUT for the Earth. I felt calm, assured, the Earth would "make it." Would wrest itself free from what was pulling it down. I began to rely on this vision, this project—a Light showing the way. A path to it. A path once there. Held for the Earth. Everything seemed so "under control," once I got this understanding.

Was it a transmission? Yes.

Once I was clued in. We only had to find it, by attuning to it. Resonating to it. Surely, enough of us would. And then more. And then more. And then, blindly, not needing to know what was going on, others would be pulled up, along, freed from the Old Earth grip. We'd make it. I was sure of it. I felt The Heart of The Light. Count on it. A Path is being held for us. It's Right There. It's Going to attract enough followers to take us all Home. In the body, not bodiless, not in physical immortality but full-bodied and full-throated, Ulysses at the homeward-bound point. We are cared for, transmitted to, with a path to aim for. A Star to steer by. I learned all this in decoding my explosion to where it was meaningful and after that realizing that Pure Light was involved. It had made itself known.

Contact reached, Sir.

Now steer the ship to its new Home.

Acknowledgments

Grateful thanks for the privilege of the experiences I've had and for whoever pushed and directed me into becoming who I am, discovering who I am, living on the level that allowed me to know myself, to know the Universe, to speak to you, to listen to you. To wake up and wonder simply: What next?

Notes

[1] Emma Woollacott, How to control a machine using your mind - BBC News.

[2] Images (Composition)," Wikipedia.

[3] Technology, Innovation, Open Mind: BBVA, March 4, 2020, Video Games Controlled by Thoughts | OpenMind (bbvaopenmind.com).

[4] Shawn Radcliffe, Experiment Shows Future Events Affect The Past - SAND (scienceandnonduality.com).

[5] Seymour Krim, *What's This Cat's Story?* (New York: Paragon House, 1991).

[6] Radcliffe, Experiment Shows Future Events Affect The Past - SAND (scienceandnonduality.com).

[7] Library of Congress, Felix Mendelssohn: Reviving the Works of J.S. Bach | Library of Congress (loc.gov).

[8] "Magnetic Resonance Imaging: MRI," https://www.nibib.nih.gov/science-education/science-topics/magnetic-resonance-imaging-mri.

[9] "Overview: Brain Tumor MRI," Mayo Clinic, https://www.mayoclinic.org/tests-procedures/mri/about/pac-20384768.

[10] Denis Le Bihan, "Diffusion MRI: What Water Tells Us about the Brain," doi: 10.1002/emmm.201404055.

[11] https://van.physics.illinois.edu/qa/listing.php?id=225.

[12] Joseph Selbie, *The Physics of God*, Kindle, Chapter 3.

[13] Selbie, *The Physics of God*, Kindle, Chapter 3: 44, 46.

[14] Craig Freudenrich and Robynne Boyd, "Neuron Structure," Neuron Structure - How Your Brain Works | HowStuffWorks.

[15] Kathryn Marie Broadhouse, "The Physics or MRI and How We Use It to Reveal the Mysteries of the Mind," https://kids.frontiersin.org/articles/10.3389/frym.2019.00023.

[16] Selbie, *The Physics of God*, Kindle, Chapter 2: 44, 45.

[17] "Quantum Field Theory," Wikipedia.

[18] "Quantum Field Theory," Britannica

[19] Selbie, *Break through the Limits of the Brain*, Kindle. Quoting in Chapter One from Lindbergh in *The Spirit of St. Louis*, 389–90.

[20] Selbie, *The Physics of God*, Kindle, Chapter 3.

[21] Anil Ananthaswamy, Aug. 4, 2010, Rethinking Einstein: The end of space-time | New Scientist.

[22] "NASA announces results of epic space-time experiment," NASA Announces Results of Epic Space-Time Experiment | Science Mission Directorate.

[23] David Cossins, June 20, 2018, The space-time echoes that point to a new theory of reality | New Scientist,

[24] Moondawg's Space News, Penn State, Oct. 14, 2021, The Warping of Space Time – Moondawg's Space News (psu.edu).

Bonus:

Go here to listen to Jef's audio comments on *Space Encounters III* rev. and *Keep This Quiet! III: Beyond* 3-D by this author.

Snippets of Reviews

Other Books by the Author

Poetry

Particle Piñata Poems

"The time of the grandmothers, of the nurturing healing feminine energy has arrived. Patriarchy has sewn destruction long enough. We must all, female and male, become healers, seers. In her epic PARTICLE PIÑATA, author Margaret Ann Harrell stands in direct lineage with the desert mystics, the poet prophets of old and, simultaneously, with the contemporary cutting edge avant-garde. In a whirling dance with the creative forces of the universe Harrell draws explicit and implicit lines to Rumi, Blake, Yeats, Joyce, Jung, and others while forging mystical connections with clouds and coastlines, dancing in the borderlands of space and time, of being and not being, of embracing and letting go. And she accomplishes it all in her own distinctly original poetic voice. Go ahead, open the front cover and enter. You'll never be the same."

—Ron Whitehead, U.S. National Beat Poet Laureate 2020–'22

"The poetry of Margaret Ann Harrell reads like a Zhuangzi of the 21st century, taking its reader through a spiritual Odyssey, where one can hear the cosmic beat in the rhythm of the word play, the pulse of heartfelt mind-blowing experiences revealing a vast span of messages from beyond. It shows the craftmanship of a female shaman who has the power to catch such a dazzling wild and free roaming content into the nets of poems. Here is a biopic in words, a biographical epic, a story of a lifetime full of surprising leaps into the story of Earth and the Cosmic Drama, a rite de passage (read the passage) initiating its reader into multiversal dimensions, bringing meaning to life where few have been looking to find it. This great bold poetry full of wit and spirit reads as a unique treat, a gift from those who know how to sow the seed for what really matters on earth: a choice to live a life guided by love and light. For those who are in love with poetry, share this genuine gift and the sheer joy of it! If you want to, go ahead!"

—Chris Van de Velde (MA Philosophy, lover of wisdom), Belgium.

The Hell's Angels *Letters:* Hunter S. Thompson, Margaret Harrell *and the* Making of an American Classic

(soft cover and limited-edition hard cover available only at Norfolk Press (https://norfolkpress.com) or through direct purchase from the author)

"Margaret Ann Harrell—in collaboration with Ron Whitehead—has assembled a dossier of all her correspondence with Thompson during the time she worked as the editor of the gonzo writer's 'strange and terrible saga of the outlaw motorcycle gangs.' Typed manuscript pages, scribbled notes, photographs, interviews, and all sorts of period ephemera relating to Hell's Angels allow the reader a valuable, behind-the-scenes glimpse into the making of this classic of New Journalism."

—Michael Dirda, the Washington Post

"Of course, there are already two collections of Hunter Thompson's letters available, but somehow they are even more enjoyable when read in the original form. Whether typed or scrawled in giant letters with a red pen, Thompson's correspondence is invariably annotated and corrected in his unique way, adding a layer of personality that was missing from the collections, as well—of course—as Harrell's explanations that provide further insight."

—David Wills, Beatdom

"A *big book, literally and figuratively* . . . The Hell's Angels Letters is a must-have text for any Hunter S. Thompson fan. Lavishly documented and illustrated with the actual correspondence that led to the publication of his breakthrough literary effort . . . The author, Margaret Harrell, who was Thompson's editor on his inaugural book, and her collaborator, Thompson's friend and associate poet Ron Whitehead, have succeeded brilliantly to create a fabulous present for you, or anyone in your life who admires Thompson's numerous achievements . . . It's worth every penny. *The* Hell's Angels *Letters: Hunter* S *Thompson, Margaret Harrell and the Making of an American Classic* gets five stars out of five! Bravo!

—Kyle K. Mann, *Gonzo Today*

Cloud Conversations & Image Stories

"Harrell's own images, striking and surprising, suggest multitudes, yielding rich new visions of figures and scenes the longer one gazes into their tufting splendor . . . Harrell's cloud photos are collaborative, between artist and nature, between beholder and photograph, between our at-a-glance perceptions and the deeper, expansive visions we tend to allow ourselves only in meditation or reverie. In inviting prefatory essays, Harrell persuasively links the art of cloud photography to 'chance' images from the history of art."

—Book Life Reviews

About Jef Crab

Belgian-born Taiji master Jef Crab lives in Suriname on the edge of the rainforest with his Surinamese family. The fear and emptiness in the eyes of children on their way to school in the early '90s shocked Jef. According to him, the cause of this was the separation on a personal, social, and environmental level. As a solution, he developed a method for restoring connectedness, the feeling that you belong to each other. In doing so, he was constantly looking for ways to make the state of optimal and connected functioning experienceable, repeatable, and transferable. Jef's efforts led to the establishment of the EcoSystem 2000 Foundation in 1994. In Suriname, several models have been developed in the field of the Earth Circle. "We are currently coordinating a regional development process for the Saamaka in Upper Suriname, at the request of the Tribal Authority. This process focuses on a nature-supporting economy integrated into the cultural reality and preserving the social structure of the indigenous Saamaka.

"Many change processes get stuck," he says, "because of inhibiting communication and tunnel vision from those surrounding or participating in the initiative /project." This is due to a lack of energy, which is why E.A.S.T Institute, which I founded, also focuses on the Human Circle. The transcultural nature and application of the method gives substance to the Celestial Circle." The Ecosystem 2000 Foundation has projects and activities worldwide, such as in Anahata Healing Centre in Ravandur (India).

About the Author

Credit: Bill Hardesty

The author of the coffee table collectible *The* Hell's Angels *Letters* in conjunction with Ron Whitehead (Norfolk Press), the *Keep This Quiet!* I–IV memoir series, as well as *Particle Pinata Poems*, the artbook *Cloud Conversations*, and a host of others, Harrell copy-edited Hunter S. Thompson's first book, *Hell's Angels*. HST acknowledged her in *Gonzo Letters* 2. She is also a book editor, cloud photographer exhibited in Europe as well as the United States, and an advanced meditation teacher in the LuminEssence school of light body and luminous body consciousness exploration, mentor to those wanting to maximize their potential. A three-time MacDowell Colony fellow, she has lived many years outside the United States— in Morocco, Switzerland (at the C. G. Jung Institute), and in Belgium. She is a sought-after speaker, for instance, multiple times at the Gonzofest in Louisville, Kentucky. Margaret is currently helping organize the Underground.

Thank You for Reading My Book

Authors live by readers and their reviews. If you enjoyed *Tricks High Up*, with an Afterword with Taiji Master Jef Crab, I would deeply appreciate an honest positive review on Amazon and/or another platform. I will read every word you write and benefit from the comments.

Thank you again and God bless.

Connect with me on Facebook. Linked In, and through my website, https://margaretharrell.com.

www.ingramcontent.com/pod-product-compliance
Lightning Source LLC
Chambersburg PA
CBHW060246030426
42335CB00014B/1607